Tongue Twisters
for
Kids

Best Joke Book For Kids
Volume 3

PETER MACDONALD

ISBN-13: 978-1494733704
ISBN-10: 1494733706

Guaranteed Good Clean Fun

Contents

So What's so Good about Tongue Twisters

They can be so much fun especially when you are with a bunch of friends.

Tongue twisters are a real challenge to say for any kid. They use similar sounding syllables, words and sounds repetitively, making it easy for anyone to trip over the words. While tongue twisters for kids can be a whole lot of fun, they also have many practical benefits to offer.

First, tongue twisters for kids can help children to begin speaking clearly. It teaches proper diction of words, since words that have repetitive sounds are difficult to say correctly without good diction. Children learn to speak more clearly when practicing with tongue twisters.

Sometimes it's hard to find good tongue twisters for your children to use. We made it easier by offering you a nice selection of tongue twisters. You'll find easy ones for younger kids, medium difficulty options and difficult tongue twisters that will challenge older kids and even adults. Let your kids have some fun with these tongue twisters as they work to improve their speech and diction at the same time.

So lets try some now!

Easy Tongue Twisters

WARNING

These Tongue Twisters are Clean, But a stumbling tongue may spill some words not intended.

.

Rubber baby buggy bumpers

.

.

Six slippery snails slowly sliding

.

.

A big box of big biscuits

.

.

Poor Pierre picked purple posies

.

Mad bunny, bad money

.

.

Unique New York

.

.

The sixth sick sheik's sheep

.

.

Fat free fruity float

Twelve tiny twins twirled twelve tiny twigs

.

.

Smelly shoes and socks

.

.

A big black bug bit a beetle

.

.

The tutor tooted the flute

.

.

Our oars are of oak

.

.

Betty better bring the butter

.

.

Baby blue bug baby black bug

.

.

Toy boat, toy boat, toy boat

.

.

The black bugs blood

.

.

Cheap sheep soup, sheep soup

.

.

Paint purple pebbles pink,

paint purple pebbles pink

.

.

Handsome Samson,

Handsome Samson,

Handsome Samson

.

.

Rooty tooty fruity,

rooty tooty fruit,

rooty tooty fruity

.

.

Angie and Annie ate all eight apples

The black bear bit a big black bug

.

.

Burglar burgles burgers,

burglar burgles burgers

.

.

Snakes silently slither,

silently snakes slither

.

.

Funny tummy,

tummy funny,

funny tummy

.

.

There's a soldier sitting on your shoulder

.

.

Double bubble bubble gum

.

.

Greek green grapes grow slow

.

.

Nine night nurses nurse nicely

Another benefit of tongue twisters for kids is that they can be used to treat speech problems. Children that have a difficult time saying certain sounds or those struggling with a lisp can benefit from using tongue twisters. Using tongue twisters even helps moms learn letter sounds correctly and word out a child's mouth muscles so they are better able to use more complicated letter sounds.

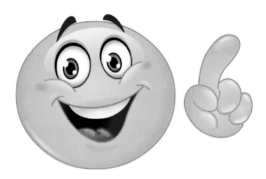

Medium Difficulty Tongue Twisters

These medium difficulty tongue twisters are great for kids age 10-11 or those who have mastered the easier tongue twisters.

.

Papa wants a proper cup

of coffee in a copper coffee cup

.

.

Crisp crusts crunchily crackle

.

.

The rain in Spain falls mainly on the plain

(from "My Fair Lady")

.

.

Who washes Washington's white woolen underwear

.

.

She sells she shells at the sea shore

.

.

A good cook could cook good

.

.

Lily loves lapping lemonade

Irish wrist watch,

Irish wrist watch,

Irish wrist watch

.

.

Sally sang seven slow sad songs slowly

.

.

Speedy Sammy the spider

spun six spiderwebs Sunday

.

.

A bit of butter Betty bought

.

.

.

Many monsters

munch monster mush

.

.

Frenchy fried

flying fish flesh

.

.

Freddy found forty-four

furry fun Furbys

We'll weather whether

the weather be fine

or whether it be hot

.

.

Yellow butter,

red jelly,

purple jam,

brown bread

.

.

Sammy sadly sold Sally's

shoes to a silly skunk

.

.

The big busy

buzzing bumble bee

bit Betty

.

.

Bitty Bobby bought a ball and bat

.

.

To use tongue twisters to their full potential, you'll want to start with easy tongue twisters. Allow them to say it slowly at first as they learn the phrase and the correct sounds. As they become more familiar with the tongue twister, then they can focus on using more speed when saying them. After you become proficient with simple tongue twisters, then you can move on to those that are a bit harder.

Difficult Tongue Twisters

Let your older children try these tongue twisters or have fun trying them yourself.

.

.

Theophilus Thistle

the unsuccessful thistle sifter

thrust three thistles

through the thick of his thumb

.

.

.

Peter Piper picked a peck of pickled peppers,

if Peter Piper picked a peck of pickled peppers,

where's the peck of pickled peppers Peter Piper
picked.

.

.

Susie sat in a shiny shoe shine shop,

she sits and she shines

and she shines and she sits

.

.

Fuzzy Wuzzy was a bear,

Fuzzy Wuzzy had no hair,

Fuzzy Wuzzy wasn't very fussy, was he?

.

.

How much wood

would a woodchuck chuck

if a woodchuck could chuck wood?

A woodchuck could chuck all the wood

he could if a woodchuck could chuck wood

.

.

The small skunk sat on a small stump

and on the stump the skunk thunk

and thunk on his stump

.

You know you need unique New York

.

.

Purple princes

and pink princesses

prance playfully around a parade

.

.

I thought I had a thought

but the thought wasn't the thought

that I thought I thought

.

.

.

Terry tickled Timmy's ticklish tummy,

when Terry tickled Timmy's ticklish tummy,

Timmy tickled Terry's tummy too

.

.

The brave brisk brigadiers

brandished bright blades and

bludgeons with bad balance

.

.

How many bright blue berries

could a bear berry carrier carry

if the bear berry carrier

could carry bright blue berries.

Betty bought a box of baking powder

to bake a batch of biscuits.

Betty places the biscuits in the basket

and took the biscuits in the basket to the bakery

.

.

Picky prickly people

pick Peter Pan peanut butter

because it's the peanut butter

that the picky prickly people pick

.

.

Sally sells her shells at the sea shore,

but if she sells her sea shells at the sea shore,

where are the sea shells Sally likes to sell

.

.

Bitty Bobby bought a bat and ball,

then Bobby use the bat

to bang the ball against the wall.

Other Books by Peter MacDonald

Best Joke Book for Kids : Best Funny Jokes and Knock Knock Jokes(200+ Jokes) Volume 1

.Best Joke book for Kids: Knock Knock Jokes 120 Good Clean Jokes Volume 2

Made in the USA
Lexington, KY
29 July 2018